BEGINNER'S MANGA
A Step-by-Step Guide

EMMETT ELVIN

Kandour Ltd

This edition printed in 2006
for Bookmart Ltd
Registered Number 2372865
Trading as Bookmart Ltd
Blaby Road
Wigston
Leicester LE18 4SE

Published by
Kandour Ltd
1-3 Colebrooke Place
London N1 8HZ
United Kingdom

2004 Kandour Ltd

10 9 8 7 6 5 4 3 2

Author and illustrator: Emmett Elvin
Cover and content design: Eugene Felder, Emmett Elvin
Page layout: Eugene Felder
Production: Karen Lomax

Printed and bound in China

ISBN 10: 1-904756-22-0

ISBN 13: 978-1-904756-22-4

CONTENTS

FOREWORD 5

Chapter 1:   INTRODUCTION AND MATERIALS 7

Chapter 2:   BODY BASICS 13

Chapter 3:   DIFFERENT FOLKS 25

Chapter 4:   HEADS, HANDS, AND FEET 37

Chapter 5:   OOK, OOK! WOOF! MEOW! 63

Chapter 6:   NONHUMAN CHARACTERS 79

Chapter 7:   OBJECTS, THINGS, AND STUFF 95

Chapter 8:   THE BIG PICTURE 109

Chapter 9:   CREATE YOUR OWN CHARACTER 119

Chapter 10: STORYTELLING 129

FOREWORD

The last couple of years have seen a huge explosion of interest in Manga, the comic art form originally from Japan. Exceptional and successful films such as Miyazaki's brilliant *Spirited Away* have only caused even greater demand for Manga and Anime, the animated version of Manga. With this boom, we've also seen a greater desire for learning this art form.

Before starting this book, I asked myself: "What kind of book would I want to see if I was just starting out?" I knew what I *wouldn't* want was page after page of dry, humorless instruction that was a chore to work through.

I've deliberately made everything in this book as transparently clear as I possibly can, but just as importantly, I hope I've made it *fun*. This book is for all who can lift a pencil and want to start turning the ideas in their heads into black-and-white reality.

Do you want to create your own characters? This book shows you how. Can you learn an easy way to draw everyday objects and make them look real? No problem. If you want to learn how to draw animals, robots, and tell stories in comic form, then it's all here.

Grab a pencil!

Emmett Elvin

5

CHAPTER 1

Introduction and Materials

What you'll need

Pencils

The most important thing is a pencil, without which you won't be able to do anything!

There are many different types. The "B" pencils have a soft lead and will produce quite a dark line. The "H" pencils are harder and make a lighter line (plus they don't wear out as quickly).

Which type you use is up to you, but a good start is an HB pencil. This is the most common kind. If it doesn't say what it is somewhere on the pencil, chances are it's an HB. It's neither hard nor soft, and erases easily.

It's really important to keep your pencil sharp all the time you're using it. The reason for this is accuracy. Also, a blunt pencil won't be able to create much detail.

At the end of this chapter, your host, Mimimi, will give you some good tips on how to get the most out of a pencil, your most important tool.

Other stuff

This book is designed to get you going as quickly as possible. But there are still a few more basic things you'll need.

You'll need some kind of eraser. There are many different kinds available, but it's best to avoid the really cheap ones as these may do little more than just smear your drawings across the page! Putty erasers are probably the best option.

You'll also need something to sharpen those pencils. But remember that there are few things worse than a blunt pencil sharpener. This will just chew and break the pencil tip and get you irritated.

OOK!

A regular sharpener like the one pictured here is fine. Just replace the blades regularly (under parental supervision if you are a minor). When you're more experienced, you can use a craft knife, which is a good sharpener.

You may find a ruler useful, although it's not essential. A long ruler is very useful if you're trying your hand at perspective.

The final tool you may want, but again, it is not essential, is something to make your artwork permanent. This involves going over your pencil lines with ink. This can be done with a wide range of tools. Brush and ink/pen and ink are common in Manga, but the beginner will probably feel more comfortable with a marker pen.

There are a huge variety of these available. Thick, thin, permanent, nonpermanent, etc. For this book, I'd recommend two permanent markers, one medium and one thick (or heavy for filling in black areas).

Using a pencil

THIS IS NOT A GOOD WAY TO HOLD A PENCIL! I'M HOLDING IT WAY TOO NEAR THE TIP. THIS MEANS IT WILL WOBBLE AND PROBABLY MAKE A LOUSY-LOOKING LINE!

THIS IS MUCH MORE LIKE IT! THIS GIVES ME MUCH GREATER CONTROL OVER THE LINE!

CHAPTER 2

Body Basics

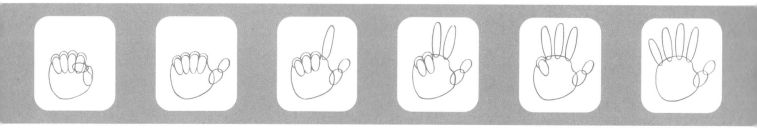

The human body

Exploring the components

If there's one thing we know we'll have to draw in our Manga, it's the human body. We can't make much progress in our storytelling without it, so let's get to it.

The simple model you'll see on the following pages gives you everything you need to get going without the need to spend ages learning complex anatomy. When you're confident drawing this way, you should devote some time to full-blown anatomy study. But for now, we'll use this easy method for getting all the basic skills for making your characters expressive and fun!

On the opposite page is a front view of this simple human body. You should be able to identify all the parts of the body listed. Try to match them up and then check the end of the chapter to see how you did!

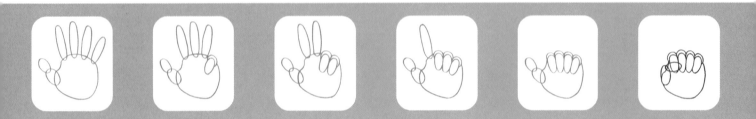

Body parts quiz

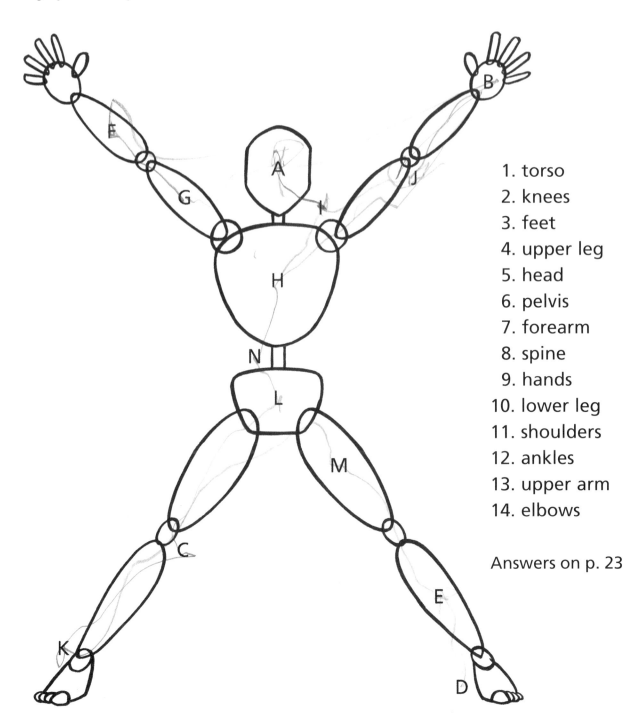

1. torso
2. knees
3. feet
4. upper leg
5. head
6. pelvis
7. forearm
8. spine
9. hands
10. lower leg
11. shoulders
12. ankles
13. upper arm
14. elbows

Answers on p. 23

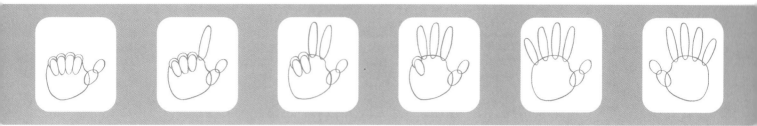

Body parts

There is one thing that makes drawing the human body a whole lot easier. It's the simple fact that we have reference material always at hand —our own bodies!

If you can't get a part of the anatomy to look right, try the same pose yourself. Are you asking your character to do something impossible? Do you understand how that part of the anatomy really works?

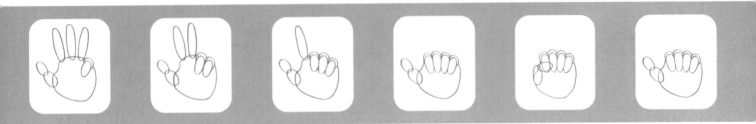

Head and neck

The shape of the head can vary quite a lot, depending on the kind of Manga we're producing. But something we have to get right no matter what the style is, is the way the neck joins the head. With a side view, the neck will never join the head at a right angle. This also makes the body look stiff, so avoid doing this!

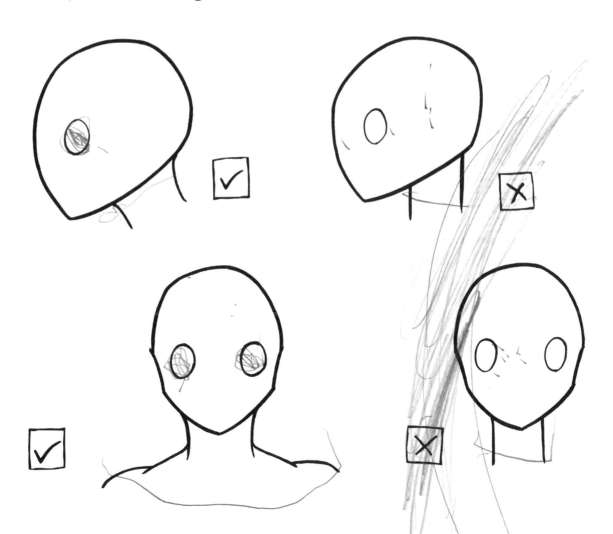

The neck should "flow" in and out of the head and shoulders, not suddenly slam into the head!

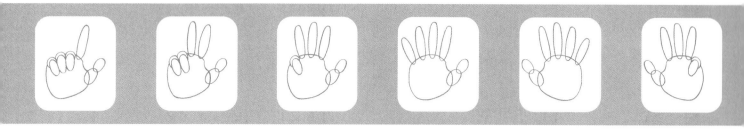

Torso and pelvis

The torso is connected to the pelvis by the spine. This gives it quite a lot of flexibility. The spine always has some amount of curve to it, even if your character's back is straight. It's this curve, if we understand it, that allows our characters to look relaxed when drawn in a standing pose.

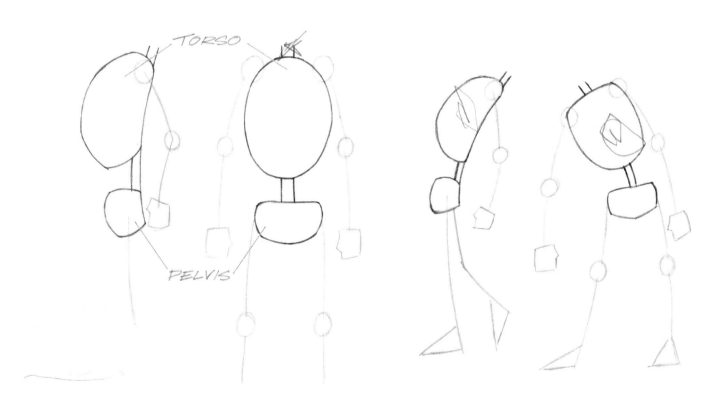

The images above show us how much the spine can bend under normal situations. Going much beyond this will probably make your character look freakish!

18

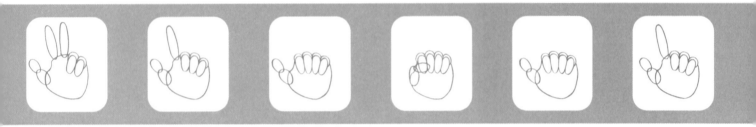

Arms and legs

The models below will give you a very simple but quite realistic basis for drawing arms and legs.

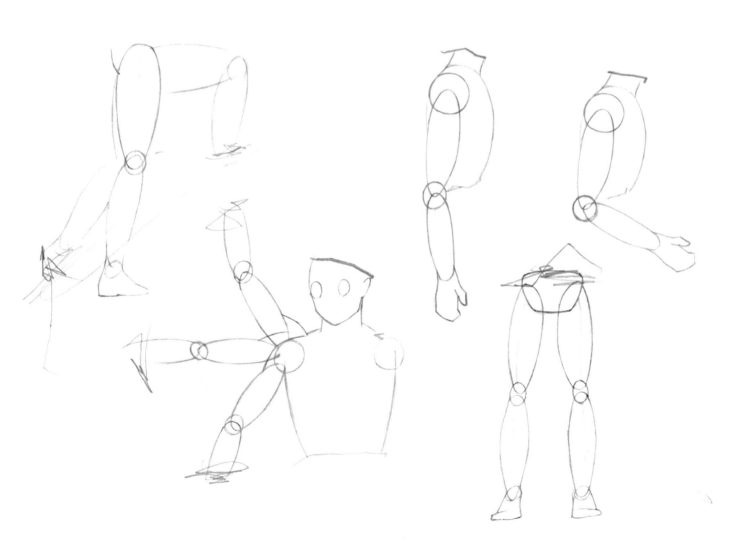

You should always establish exactly where the knees and elbows are before drawing the actual limbs. Get this right and it will save you a lot of time!

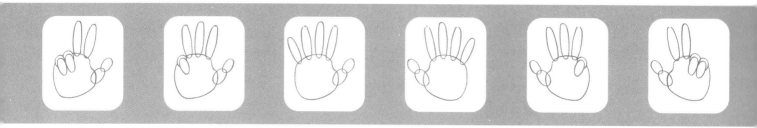

The body in action

The sketches on these two pages are to show you that you can draw your character in lots of different poses, and quickly.

Use the body model on page 15 and draw as quickly as you can. Either copy the drawings here or make up some of your own—or both!

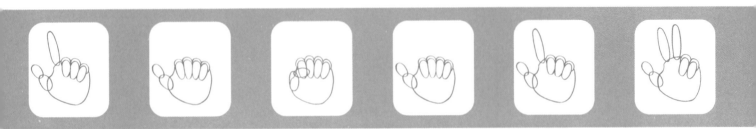

If a pose starts to go wrong, stop drawing it and start again. Draw the same pose fifty times if necessary. If you work this way, and don't get caught up in details, your drawing ability will rapidly improve.

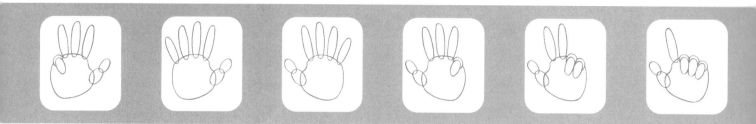

Body do's and don'ts

It sounds like a simple thing to draw, but drawing a standing figure can be really tough, especially side on. Below are some common mistakes.

THIS IS THE RIGHT WAY TO DRAW SOMEONE STANDING! THE SPINE HAS A SLIGHT CURVE TO IT AND THE BODY LOOKS BALANCED AND RELAXED.

THIS IS THE WRONG WAY TO DRAW SOMEONE STANDING! THE SPINE IS NEVER COMPLETELY STRAIGHT—IT CURVES IN ONE DIRECTION OR THE OTHER.

Of course, it's all too easy to go over the top on your spine curve, too. On the right is an example. It's an exaggeration, but it can happen! So watch out!

Here is the other extreme. Again, it is an exaggeration, but serves to illustrate the awkwardness created by curving the spine in the wrong direction.

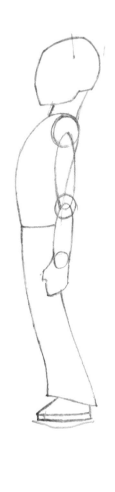

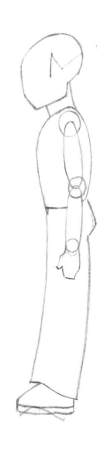

PAGE 15 QUIZ ANSWERS!

1. torso H
2. knees C
3. feet D
4. upper leg M
5. head A

6. pelvis L
7. forearm F
8. spine N
9. hands B
10. lower leg E

11. shoulders I
12. ankles K
13. upper arm G
14. elbows J

CHAPTER 3

Different Folks

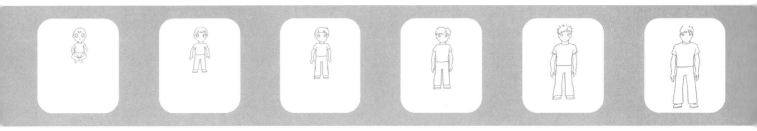

Proportions

Man, child, or baby?

One common mistake we tend to make when starting to draw is to make adults no more than bigger versions of kids, or vice versa.

In reality, different parts of the body grow at different rates. This means when we are babies, we have big heads, small bodies, and small arms and legs. As we grow older, our heads don't get that much bigger but our bodies and particularly our arms and legs get much bigger.

Have a look at the drawings on these two pages. They'll give you an idea of how the parts of the body change in relationship to one another, with age.

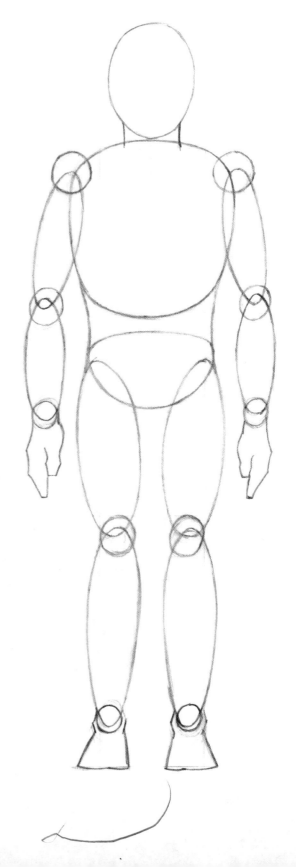

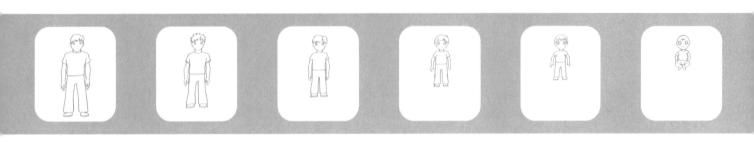

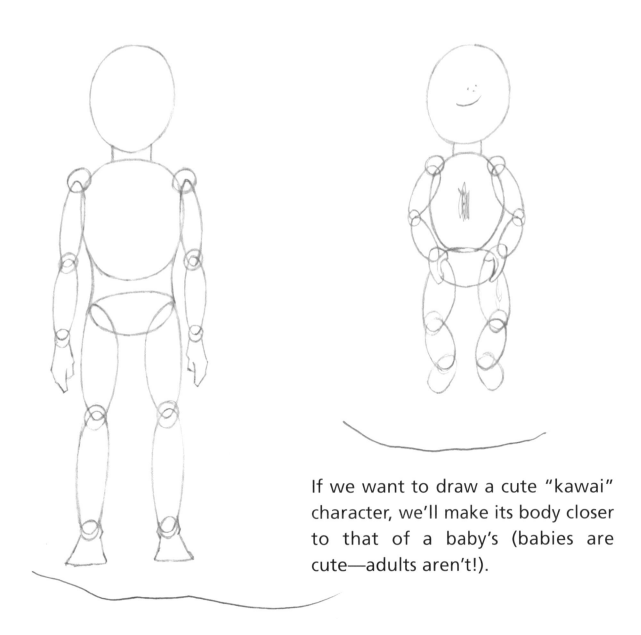

If we want to draw a cute "kawai" character, we'll make its body closer to that of a baby's (babies are cute—adults aren't!).

If we want to draw someone in a position of authority, we would use proportion much more similar to that of the adult on the facing page.

Try experimenting with just the basic shapes, as above. You'll soon get an idea of what looks "adult" and what looks "babyish."

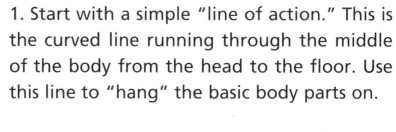

Adult male

1. Start with a simple "line of action." This is the curved line running through the middle of the body from the head to the floor. Use this line to "hang" the basic body parts on.

2. Before we get involved with any details on the anatomy, it's a good idea to establish where the clothes will be.

We'll dress him in a good suit.

GROWN-UP MEN HAVE WIDE SHOULDERS, THICK NECKS, AND BIG HANDS AND FEET. WE'LL SEE THE DIFFERENCE FROM GROWN-UP WOMEN IN TWO PAGES!

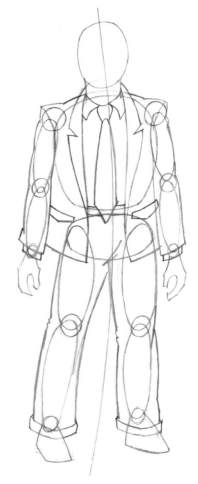

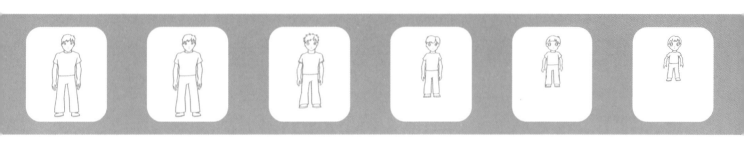

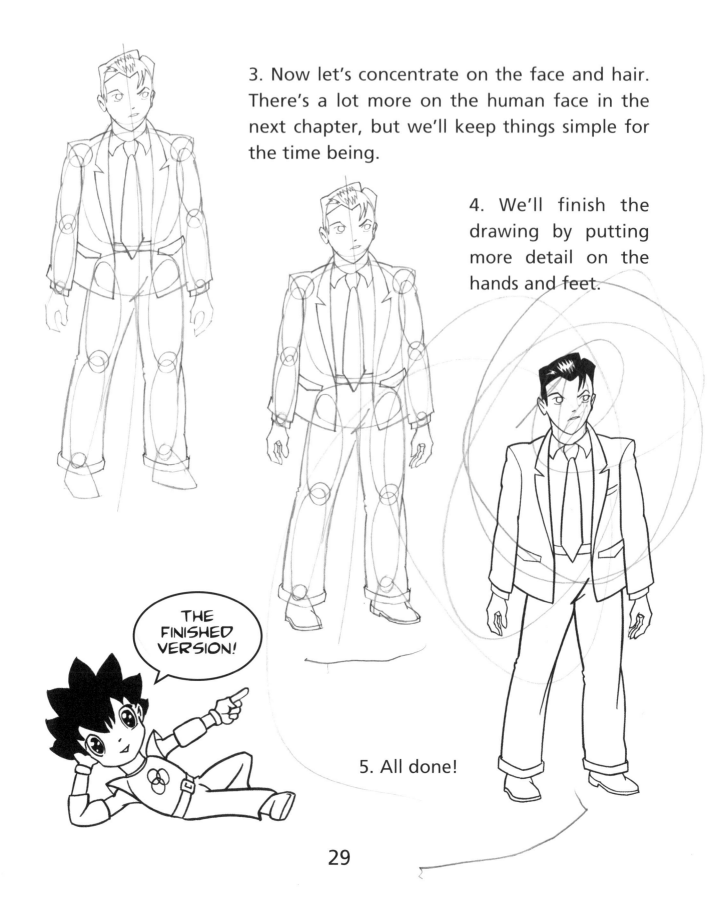

3. Now let's concentrate on the face and hair. There's a lot more on the human face in the next chapter, but we'll keep things simple for the time being.

4. We'll finish the drawing by putting more detail on the hands and feet.

THE FINISHED VERSION!

5. All done!

Adult female

1. The line of action is like a pulled-out "S" shape—women tend to be a lot more curvy than men!

2. As before, hang the basic body parts as above. Then add a pocketbook for fun.

3. Now draw details on the upper body, hair, face, and chest.

30

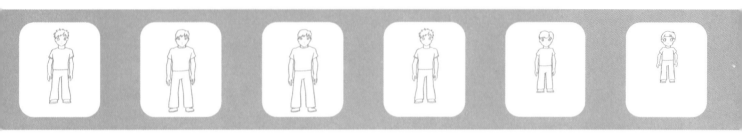

4. The last details we'll add are: skirt line, shoe details, cuffs, neckline, necklace, and more pocketbook detail.

CAN YOU SEE HOW THAT ORIGINAL SHAPE IS STILL IN THE FINAL IMAGE?

5. If you've inked your drawing, leaving out the guidelines you don't need, it should look similar to the final image here.

Teenage boy

Although this teenage boy is not far off from adult height, he still has some filling out to do. His shoulders are closer together and his chest is less developed.

1. The line of action here is similar to the adult male. We're going to have him holding a soccer ball, which covers up most of his forearm and right hand.

2. Next, we need to add some clothes. We'll give him a loose-fitting T-shirt and trousers, and a pair of sneakers.

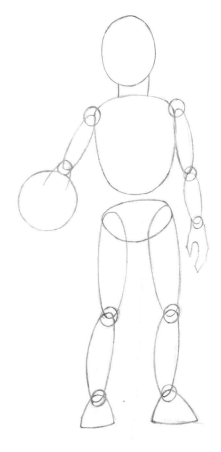

SEE HOW HIS CLOTHES ROUGHLY FOLLOW HIS BODY SHAPE? IN SOME PLACES THE MATERIAL "HANGS," IN OTHERS IT "BUNCHES."

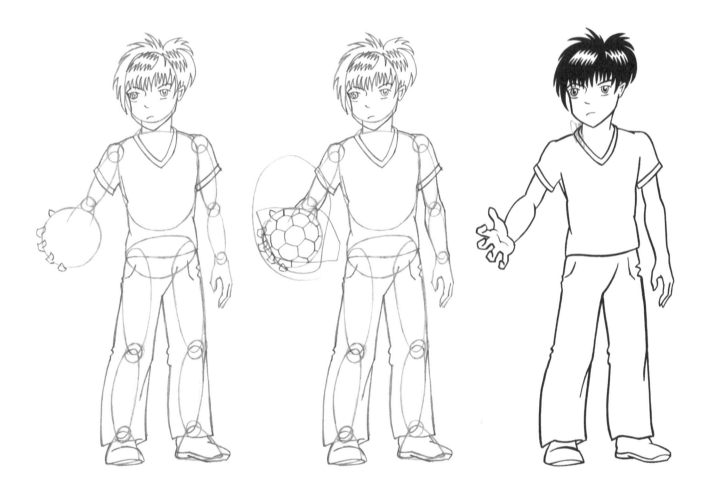

3. Next, let's work on his head and show where his fingers are gripping the ball. If you don't feel confident with his hair highlights, keep them simple for now. There's more about this in the next chapter.

4. Put the details on the ball. Try and get the lines to follow the ball's shape.

5. If you want to, finish the drawing in ink and erase the old pencil lines.

33

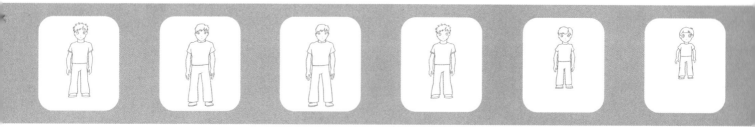

Teenage girl

Like the teenage boy, this girl is yet to "fill out." This means her hips aren't as wide and her upper body is a little less well-developed.

1. The line of action here is similar to the adult female on page 30. It follows the curve of her spine and the pelvis angle.

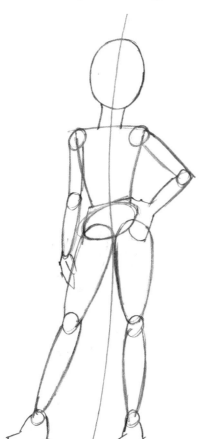

2. When you're happy with the body shape, dress her very simply in a V-neck shirt, skirt, and shoes.

3. Now for the detail on the face and hair: Let the hair flow, following the shape of her head. The face isn't too important at this stage. There is a lot more information about that coming up in chapter 4.

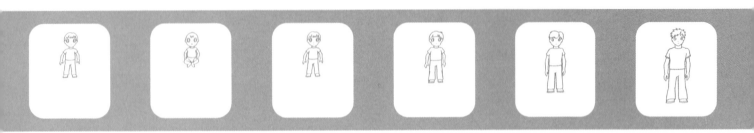

4. Even if you're going to ink the drawing, it's still a good idea to "clean up" a little. This should make sure you don't accidentally ink the wrong lines!

IF YOU'RE HAVING TROUBLE WITH THE POSE, TRY THINKING ABOUT THE BODY'S WEIGHT ON HER HIP. IS SHE WELL BALANCED?

5. All done!

CHAPTER 4

Heads, Hands, and Feet

Heads

Getting emotional

The faces to our right show a wide variety of emotions. Fear, happiness, tiredness, anger, and many, many more expressions can be created with just a few simple lines.

We can completely change the attitude of our characters by only very small changes. For instance, face (a) and face (c) are only different in the way the eyebrows are drawn. Yet face (a) looks happy and relaxed while face (c) looks evil and scheming.

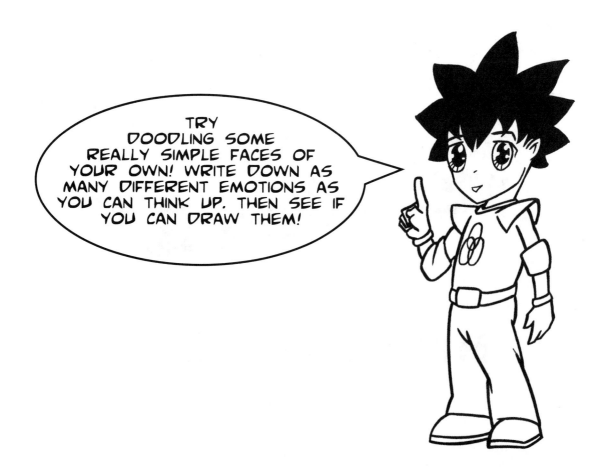

38

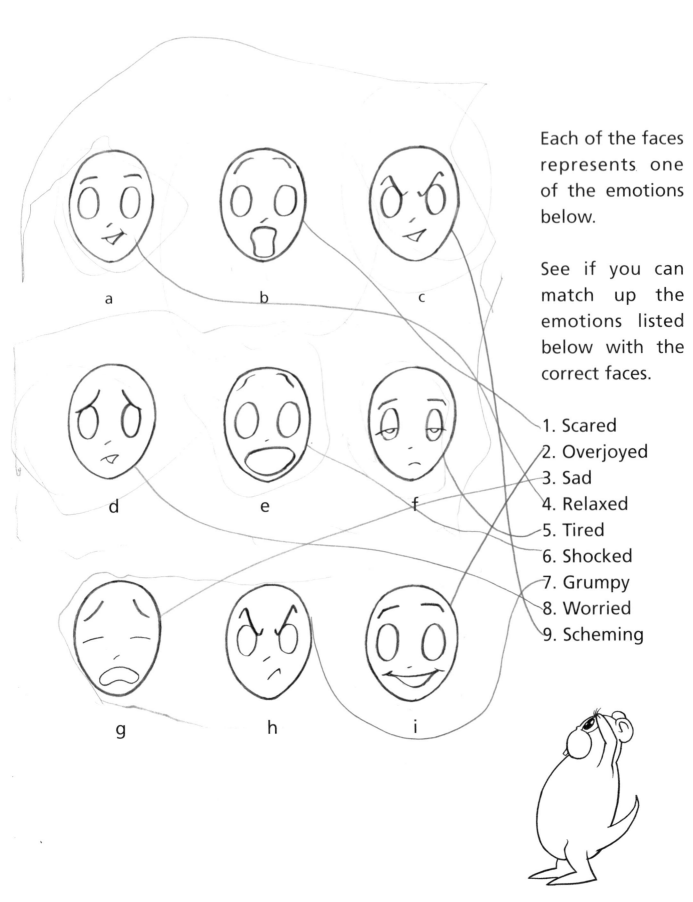

a

b

c

d

e

f

g

h

i

Each of the faces represents one of the emotions below.

See if you can match up the emotions listed below with the correct faces.

1. Scared
2. Overjoyed
3. Sad
4. Relaxed
5. Tired
6. Shocked
7. Grumpy
8. Worried
9. Scheming

Head shapes

There's a huge range of head shapes in Manga, from the classic "doll's head" shape, which is typical of *shoujo / shounen* Manga, through to the more realistic styles in the more grown-up Manga and much of Anime.

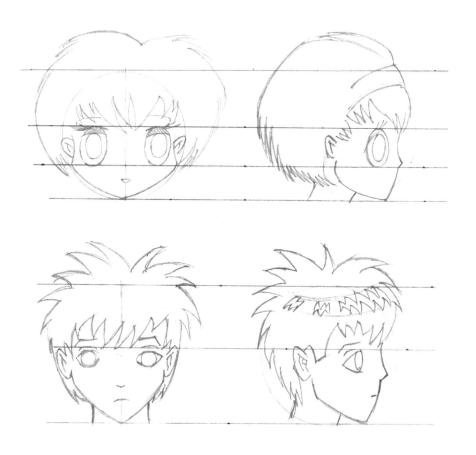

These two pages show some head styles. The shape you choose for your characters depends on several factors, including the type of Manga you're creating and simple personal preference.

The top face is typical *shoujo* Manga—a squashed head, made for maximum width to fit those big, gooey eyes into. She is a *kawai* girl: Her eyes and nose are just small dots. With this style, they're sometimes not there at all!

The middle face is more typical of an Anime style. The hallmarks of this style are a sharply pointed chin and enclosed eyes.

The bottom face is the opposite of the kawai girl at the top. His flat-top hair and mighty chin tell us this guy is serious! His head is very nearly a rectangle!

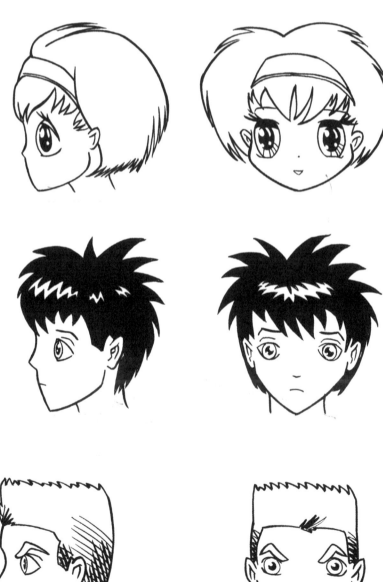

41

Three different head views

Head on

To help you get started with heads and understand the principles involved, the next few pages show a number of different heads. It's a good idea to start by copying at least one of them. Once you think you've got the hang of what's involved, try drawing the same head but at a slightly different angle. Then try changing the features slightly.

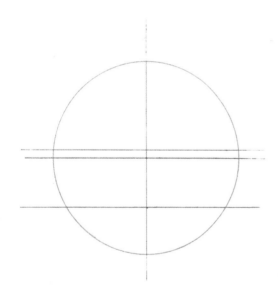

Step 1. A simple circle is our starting point for a head. Draw a line through the center from left to right and another line through the center from top to bottom. Draw another line slightly above the first line as shown and one more about 3/4 of the way down the center line.

Step 2. The lines we've just drawn are the eye, ear, and nose lines. The reason for this much accuracy is that we'll use exactly the same guidelines for the other heads we'll be drawing. Draw two ovals within the eye guides and add a small nose, as shown.

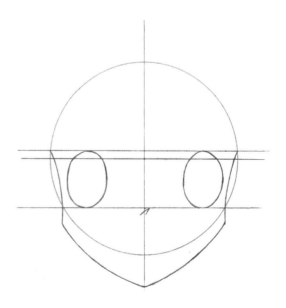

Step 3. Now for the ears. Get the outline shape right first and make sure one ear is a mirror image of the other. Put the mouth in around the point where the circle and vertical line meet.

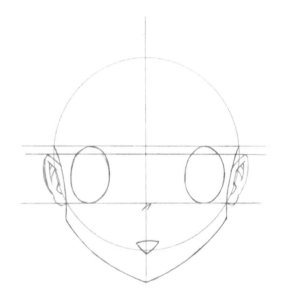

Step 4. Our girl wouldn't be very Manga without a good head of hair. You can either use your own style or copy this one. But the first thing you should think about is the overall shape.

Step 5. Finally, we add the detail to the eyes. Give her some eyelashes, making them fan out as shown. Add some eyebrows and then the eye details. Lastly, put in the black areas of her eyes. She's cute!

Head in profile

Most people starting out drawing find this harder than the "head on" pose. Pay particular attention to the angle of the jawline and the shape of the skull.

Step 1. Start with the basic circle and lines as explained in step one on page 42.

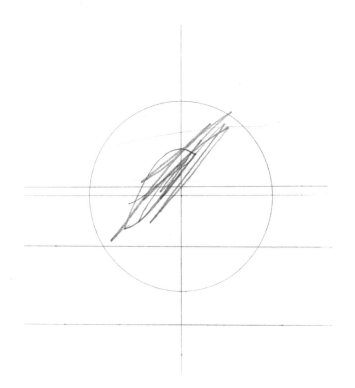

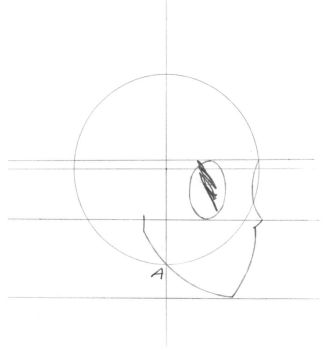

Step 2. Draw the eye 2/5 of the way in to the left semicircle, just like on the right. Use the top eyeline as a starting point for her nose. Draw an arc from this point down to the nose line. Form the under part of the nose as shown, then draw another arc down to the chin line. Draw one more arc through point A.

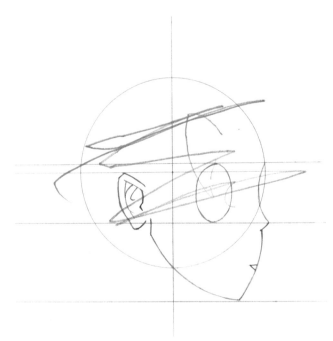

Step 3. Draw her ear just behind where you finished the jawline. Add her mouth at a point level with the bottom of the circle.

Step 4. When you put in her hair, make sure it's the same height as the previous drawing on page 43.

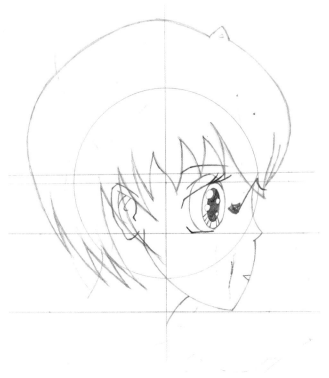

Step 5. As with the previous drawing on page 43, add the eye detail. That's it!

45

Three-quarter view

Step 1. This is the hardest to master, but the principle is exactly the same. Start with the same template, but draw a line as in the picture on the right. It should divide the right half of the circle in half again.

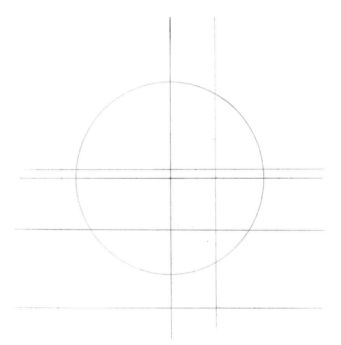

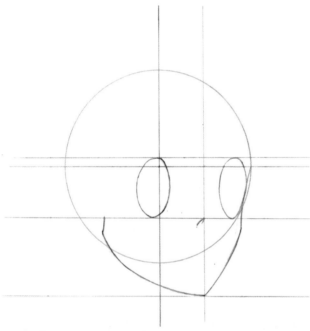

Step 2. This line is the midpoint between the eyes, where the nose should be. Put them in as shown. Then add the jawline. The chin also sits on this line.

Step 3. Put the mouth on the same center line as the nose. The ear sits on the left edge of the circle, like so.

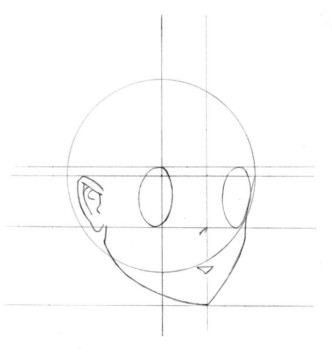

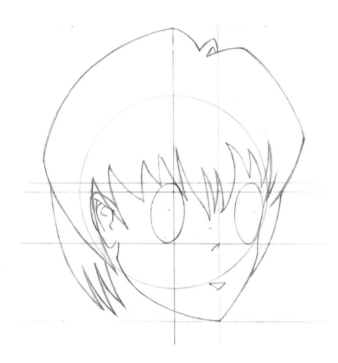

Step 4. If you've done the two previous heads, her hair should contain something of both styles. Refer back to step four for those two heads and compare it with this one. See what I mean?

Step 5. All that remains to draw are the eye details.

If this is giving you real trouble, try working first with just the eyes. When you're happy you've got the understanding, introduce the other parts of the face. If you still can't get it right, try simplifying the face and hair, working in more detail as your confidence grows.

WORK YOUR WAY THROUGH THESE HEADS! BY THE TIME YOU'RE DONE, YOU'LL PROBABLY BE ABLE TO MAKE UP YOUR OWN!

Hair

A little or a lot

How many ways are there to draw hair? Pretty much as many as you can think of! The first thing we need to consider is the level of detail we want to put into our character's hair.

The two following pictures show the same head and hairstyle. The first is drawn very simply.

The level of detail you choose depends partly on the amount of detail in the rest of the drawing. Really simple hair on a very detailed face will look out of place.

Notice that the hair in the drawing above all grows out of a central point.

The two pictures above show how the hair follows the shape of the head. It starts at the crown (the top part of the head where the tufts are clearly visible) and flows outward from there.

These two pictures show the effect of light reflecting off dark hair. See how the highlights really follow the head shape?

Try drawing a simple head and then drawing lines from the crown that follow the head shape. Then use these lines to "map out" the hair.

More about hair

Once we've got the hang of surface detail, the other thing we need to think about is *volume*. By this I mean the amount of hair. And not just the length, but also the thickness. Manga hair is notorious for its volume. Certain artists seem to have contests between themselves to see who can create the biggest hairdo.

For now, though, let's look at a simple way to draw a full head of long hair and get it right every time. Once again the secret is in the planning.

Don't even think about individual strands until you've got the basic shape worked out. Then you can get busy with the detail.

Long hair—side view

Use the same approach for the side view. Then feel free to add loads more detail, hair strands, etc. Go wild!

We've now covered everything you need to know about drawing heads. Although heads have the most parts to draw, they're not actually the most complex part of the body to draw.

So what is the most difficult to draw? That's coming up next.

Hands

The basics

If you ask people who are starting out in the world of drawing what gives them the most problems, they'll probably say hands. With a few simple guidelines, we can stop being scared of them and start having fun drawing them. There are really three areas involved. These are: the palm, the fingers, and the thumb.

1. Of course, the palm isn't really a circle, but it will do to get us started.

2. So what are these funny lines fanning out from the bottom of the palm? If you look at the back of your hand and spread your fingers, you'll see something very similar. These are the tendons, the "cables" that help operate your fingers.

3. These tendon lines help us establish the position of the fingers. Now we can draw a line to show the length of the outstretched fingers. This line doesn't quite follow the line of the circle. Why not?

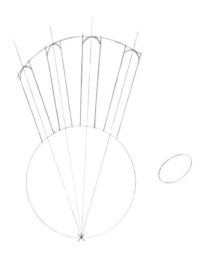

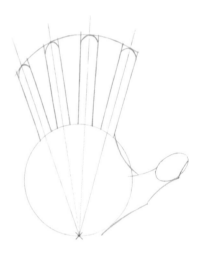

4. When we draw in the fingers, we can see this curved line represents their different lengths. We'll also put an oval shape in to show the position of the thumb.

5. There's no really easy method for drawing the thumb. This is mainly because it moves around so much. It's much less "fixed" than the fingers.

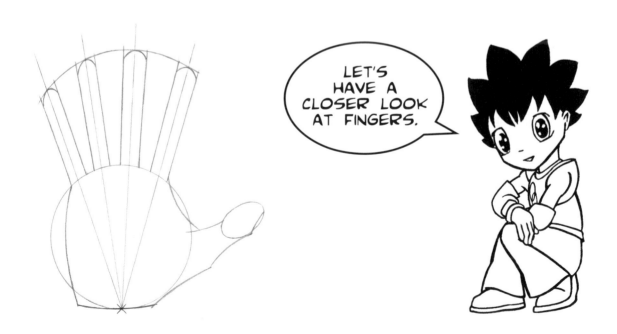

LET'S HAVE A CLOSER LOOK AT FINGERS.

Fingers and thumbs

The fingers are a collection of four independent multijointed objects. No wonder they are hard to draw! Let's try and make life a little easier for ourselves. Here's a close look at the forefinger. Pay close attention to the way it is constructed.

As the picture on the left shows, the finger is made up from one knuckle and two joints. These connect three bones. The top two joints can't move left or right, but the knuckle can.

The picture to our right shows all the knuckles and joints involved in drawing the fingers. Knowing where all these appear helps us with the shape of the fingers and the whole hand.

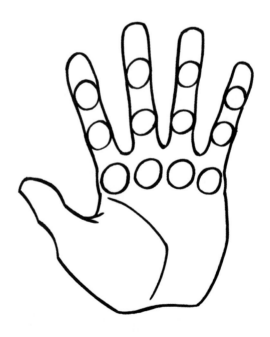

The thumb

The picture on the right shows the joints of the thumb. It has one less joint than a finger, but makes up for this by being much more free moving.

The structure of the thumb is so different from the fingers that it's almost impossible to work out an easy formula for drawing it.

Another way

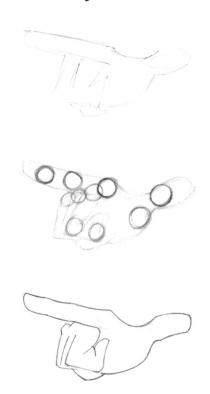

The method of drawing the hand in steps one to three below is a different approach.

Step 1. Doodle a quick sketch, roughly representing the shape of the hand you want to draw.

Step 2. Carefully work out where the knuckles and joints should be.

Step 3. Use the knuckles and joints to "connect the dots."

Hands in poses

If you're really stuck for a hand pose, you may find something close on these two pages that you can copy.

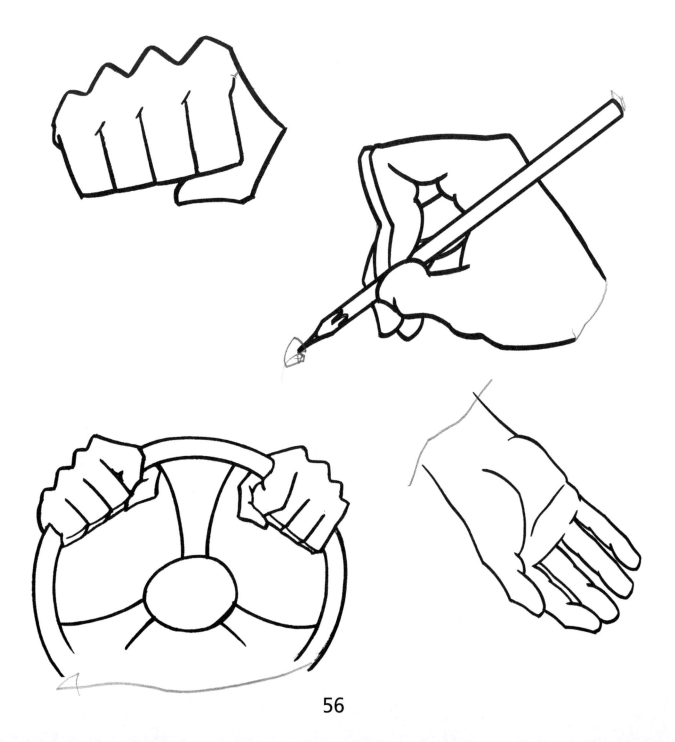

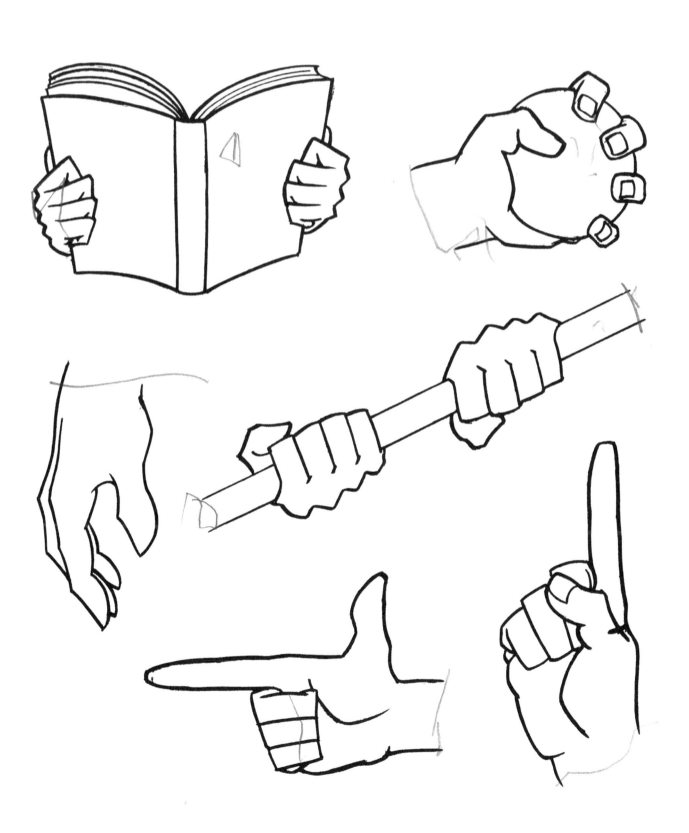

Basic feet and shoes

Simple construction

Although the feet appear simpler than the hands, they can be even more difficult to make convincing. Strangely, it's incredibly easy to get them wrong, so let's take a look at their construction, keeping things as simple as possible.

The two large circles on the soles of the feet below represent the heel and the ball of the foot. Getting these positioned correctly will go a long way to helping us draw good feet and shoes.

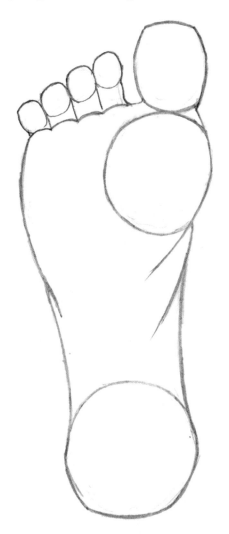
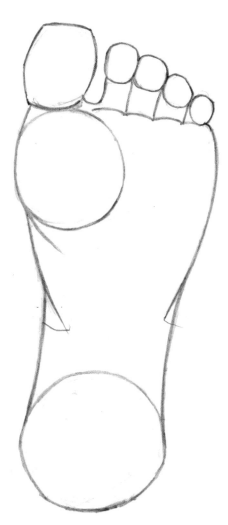

The heel and good balance

The heel should always be slightly farther back than the ankle. If not, your character may look as if it is on the verge of falling backward. For this reason, the heel is a very important part of making your character appear well-balanced.

The ankle is made up of two bones that stick out at the point where the leg joins the foot. The inside ankle bone is lower and slightly bigger. We can treat the four small toes as one object, as these are hardly ever shown moving separately.

Drawing shoes

As you can see from the drawings below, the basic shoe shape is a simpler version of the foot. This is more obvious in the drawing of the soles.

Practice drawing this simple boot shape from the angles shown below. Then, try some other angles of your own until you have the hang of it. Make sure you draw the beginning of the leg, too. This is a good way of making sure your boot will work with a human attached.

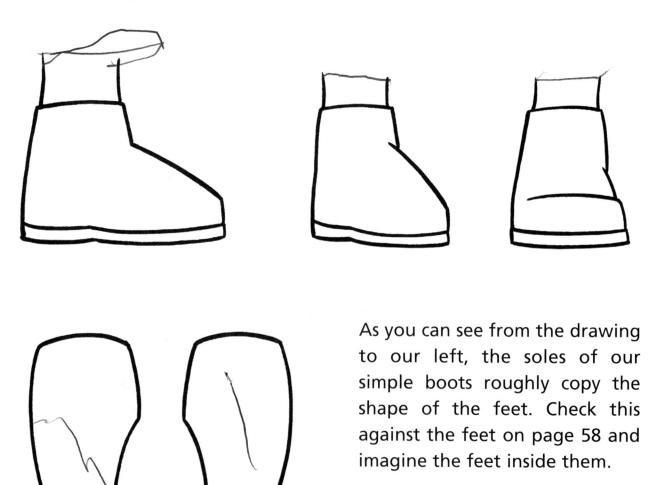

As you can see from the drawing to our left, the soles of our simple boots roughly copy the shape of the feet. Check this against the feet on page 58 and imagine the feet inside them.

Once you feel you've mastered the basic boot, you can add other features. Start by getting the ankles right. When you're happy with that, add some details to the shoe, such as a strap, tongue, laces, etc.

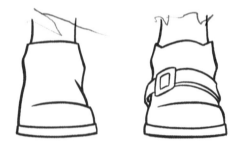

The bottom drawing shows the boots in action. This can take a while to get right. As always, start with the simplest shape and add details as your confidence grows.

We've now covered the whole of the human body in some detail. You should now be able to draw characters on at least a basic level. If you really want to get good, though, real-life reference is the way to go. The more you do this, the more you'll notice new things about the human figure you never realized. But next, it's the turn of the animals.

CHAPTER 5

Ook, Ook!
Woof! Meow!

Drawing animals

They're not human!

Cats can fly. People turn into pigs. Dogs speak better than their masters. Well, at least in Manga they do, so we'd better learn how to draw them.

There are two things to immediately think about. What makes animals different from us? What makes them similar?

As you can see in the image below, other mammals have the same basic parts as us. The main difference is they walk on four legs instead of two. Also, their heads come in many shapes and sizes.

If you can start to picture mammals in this way, you'll start to see a basic pattern common to all mammals. All mammal bodies are variations on the same theme.

Fido for beginners

What is a dog made of?

Shown here are all the shapes we need to draw a dog. They're the right shapes for drawing a dog seen from the side.

See if you can see where the parts go (before looking at the drawing below).

The parts are: Tail, body, neck, head, muzzle, nose, upper back leg, lower back leg, front leg and paws (front and back).

This is how our dog should look if we've put all the parts together in the correct way.

If you want to try an experiment, copy the drawing above, cut out all the different parts, and then put your dog together.

You could even try repositioning the way the dog stands.

Now we know where the basic shapes of our dog are. Let's make him look more like a dog and less like a balloon animal!

The gray lines show our old drawing. What we do now is use only the lines we need in order to draw the real dog. We also add important details such as ears, eyes, a mouth, and toes. The drawings below show a dog drawn from the front using the same method.

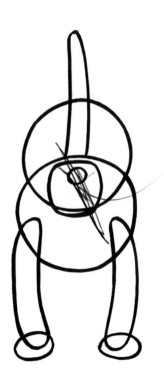

Drawing a dog: part 2

Now that we've come to grips with the most simple way to construct a dog, let's try a more advanced way of doing things.

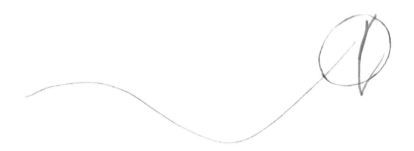

Step 1. Draw a line of action that shows the basic shape of the dog. Add an oval to show the position of the head.

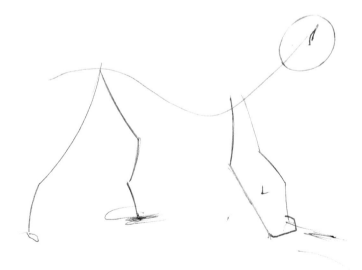

Step 2. Draw the position and shape of the legs, as shown.

Step 3. Indicate the chest area with a large oval. Use circles to indicate the leg joints.

Step 4. Now that we have the framework, we can put some flesh on the bones. Then add the tail and the dog's snout, as shown.

Step 5. First erase the guidelines you no longer need. Next, add the final details. These are mainly the face and a hint of fur in key places.

Step 6. The final, inked dog!

Meow's the time

Drawing felines

If Fido is loyal, hungry, and noisy, then our feline friends are sleek, agile, and independent. How can we work these qualities into our drawings of cats?

When trying to get new ideas about animals, it's a good idea to just work up a few quick doodles. These are done without the usual principles of construction and are put straight down on the page as expressively as possible. Here's an example:

Although the doodle is probably not that accurate, it does have the quality of "catness." The arched back, the vertical tail, and the stick-up fur all help to communicate the idea of "cat."

Draw that cat!

TYPICAL CAT! LEAPING ELEGANTLY FROM A SHED ROOF TO THE NARROW EDGE OF A FENCE, AND USING ITS TAIL FOR BALANCE.

Step 1. We need the basic shape and body parts of the cat to start us off.

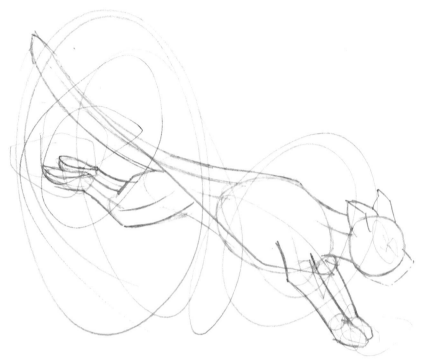

Step 2. Now to flesh out the body. See how the line from the cat's shoulder to the tip of its tail is one long, gentle curve?

Step 3. Now for the details: Eye, nose, whiskers, and mouth. And neaten up any untidy bits.

The final cat

THE CAT'S CHEST IS ABOUT TWICE AS DEEP AS ITS TUMMY AREA! THIS LEAPING POSITION REALLY SHOWS THIS OFF.

Step 4. The finished image. A clean, simple expression of a cat. If you're happy with your drawing, you could try doing a long-haired version!

Monkey business

Go ape!

Chimps, gorillas, and the other higher apes are our closest relatives. This means they have more in common physically with humans than any other animals on the planet.

However, this doesn't mean they are just humans who drag their knuckles on the ground. Their bodies are covered in long hair and their faces only vaguely resemble ours.

As they spend a great deal of their lives living in trees, their upper bodies are built for this way of life. Their arms and hands are powerful and longer than our own.

Ook! Ook!

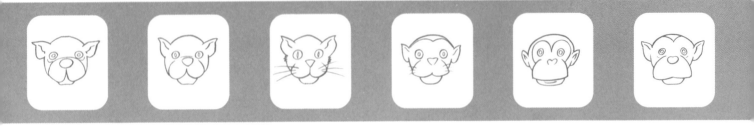

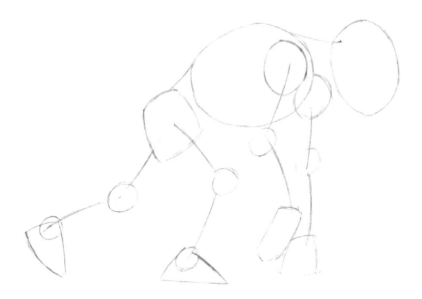

Step 1. The first step is to work out our ape's pose with a few simple lines. Show the position of all the joints.

Step 2. Now to flesh out the form of the body—it's starting to look like an ape!

Step 3. Let's get to work on that head. It's a good idea to start with the ape's distinctive "muzzle," the cup-shaped part containing the mouth and nose. Get this right and the rest should follow.

Step 4. Now that everything should be in place, we'll sharpen up any last details. Finally, here's a great technique for adding form to creatures with a lot of body hair. We can use the ape's hair to describe its shape and form. See how the pencil lines follow the ape's shape?

Step 5. When you have inked your ape, it should look a bit like this one!

OOK!
OOK!

In this chapter, we've looked at some simple and some not so simple ways of creating animals. Which method you use is up to you, but you'll probably end up using a combination of both.

Remember, start simple and make sure all the basics are strong and clear. Then, when you know the drawing really works, you can add the detail.

CHAPTER 6

Nonhuman
Characters

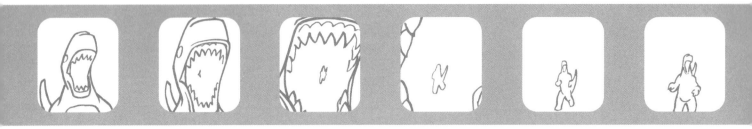

Robots and monsters

Not so human

In this chapter, we're going to have a look at some characters that are neither animals nor humans.

They're all big guys (or gals), so they need to look powerful and maybe even a little bit scary. So how do we achieve this?

Back in chapter two we talked about proportion. Remember how the difference in size between the head and body tells us about the size of the person? Well, we can use this to help us create something *really* big.

Have a look at the two images below. Although they're the same size, one of them has the proportions of a much larger person.

If the human body didn't stop growing at around eighteen years of age, but carried on until it was eight feet tall, it would look a bit like the drawing on the right.

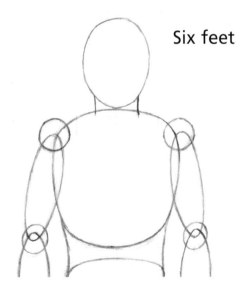
Six feet

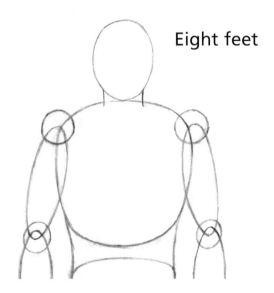
Eight feet

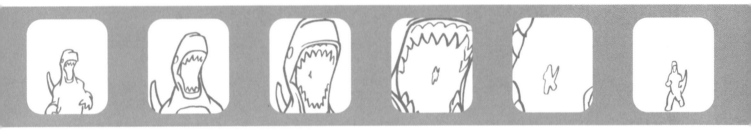

Giants

What else might add a feeling of size to our giant humanoids? Using the same idea, we know that as a boy grows into a man, his shoulders become wider. So, if he didn't stop growing, he'd have *extremely* wide shoulders!

Look at the drawing on the left to see what we've got so far as our model for giant characters.

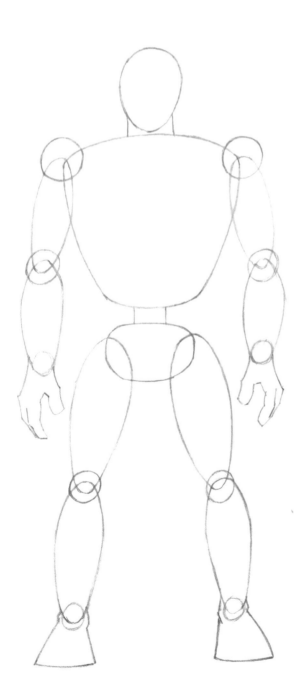

I think you'll agree, that is a very big and powerful-looking character frame!

Now that we understand size and power better, let's try and put these ideas together and create something colossal.

The following pages teach you to draw robots and monsters.

81

Giant mech warrior

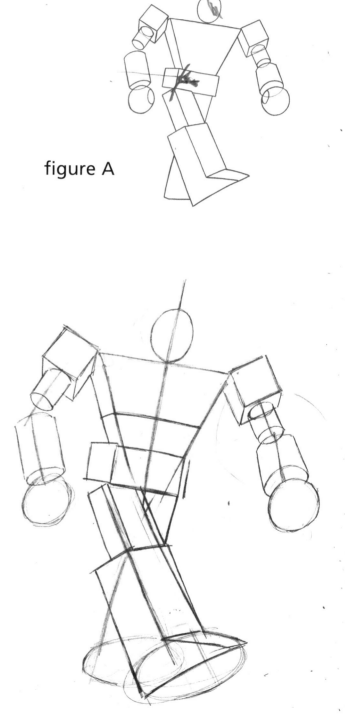

figure A

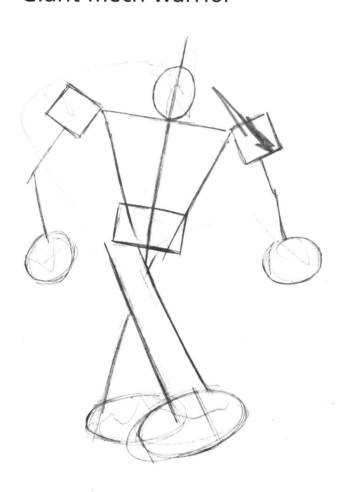

Step 1. The line of action is at a slight angle, but straight. "Block out" the major body parts.

Step 2. The whole body is made from simple geometric shapes. You can see this more clearly in figure A.

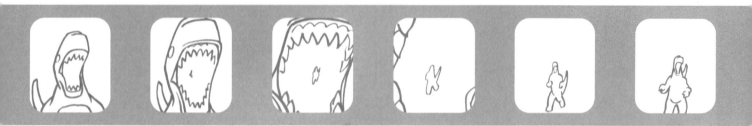

Step 3. Add some headgear, define the hands, and add some detail to the boots. Add the shoulder connector rods.

Step 4. Tidy it up!

IF YOU'RE REALLY HAVING TROUBLE, TRY WORKING OUT THE INDIVIDUAL PARTS FIRST!

83

Final detail

Step 5. This is why I asked you to tidy up. We have to add quite a bit of detail at this stage. Add all the final details to his torso, boots, and head.

Step 6. Add the details on the arms and shoulders. Now your warrior is ready to be inked!

WHEN DOING THIS MUCH DETAIL, WORK LIGHTLY AT FIRST, AS THERE WILL PROBABLY BE SOME ERASING TO BE DONE!

Draw a dragon!

NO, IT'S NOT A PIECE OF STRING! THAT LINE'S GOING TO BE A DRAGON!

Step 1. Manga dragons are a lot more snakelike than Western-style ones. Get a good, snaky shape to start with.

Step 2. Using the line of action as a center guide, add some body mass. Indicate the position of the head.

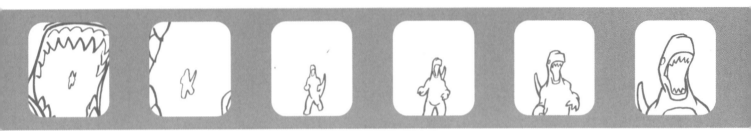

Step 3. For the legs, we have to imagine a cross between a lizard and an eagle. Be careful where you place the feet.

Step 4. Now for the trickiest part, the head. Start by placing the eye correctly and work everything else around that.

Cleanup and final detail

Step 5. This is a good time to erase that original line of action. We need to create two new ones for the dragon's mane and scales.

Step 6. See how its mane follows the new line off its back and along its tail? The line for its scales follows a very similar path.

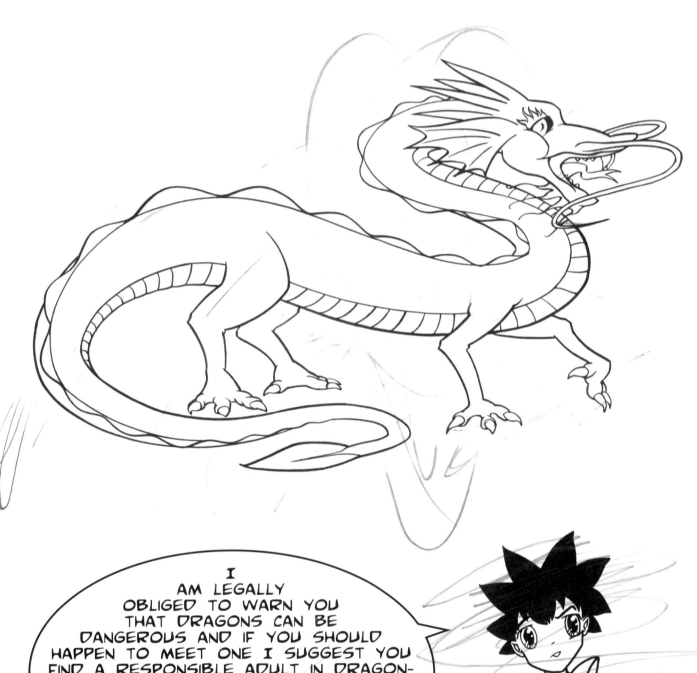

I AM LEGALLY OBLIGED TO WARN YOU THAT DRAGONS CAN BE DANGEROUS AND IF YOU SHOULD HAPPEN TO MEET ONE I SUGGEST YOU FIND A RESPONSIBLE ADULT IN DRAGON-RESISTANT BODY ARMOR. SERIOUSLY, THOUGH, IF YOU'VE MANAGED TO DRAW THE LAST TWO CHARACTERS, YOU'VE CONQUERED TWO OF THE TOUGHEST THINGS IN THIS BOOK!

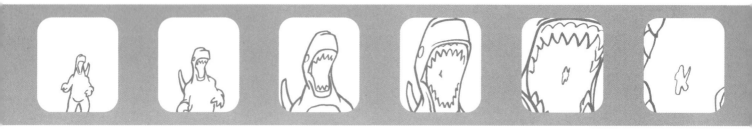

Destroyer of cities!

Nothing causes carnage quite like a fifty-foot-high prehistoric maniac lizard. Even so, there's something quite cute about one on a rampage.

Step 1. Draw the line of action and an oval indicating the position of the head.

For the next steps, make sure you draw a complete oval. This will ensure that all the parts connect.

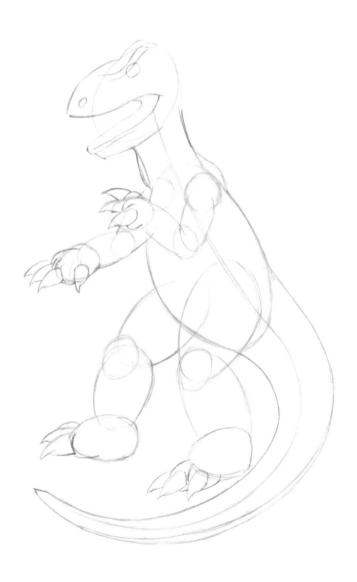

Step 2. Add the large oval for the body first, then the arms, the legs, and the neck.

Step 3. Use the original line of action as a center guide for the tail. Add the head details and fingernails.

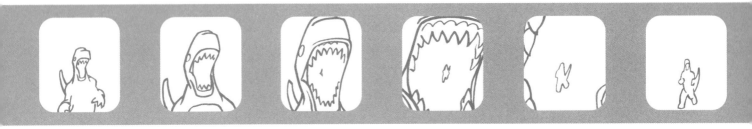

Nearly finished . . .

Step 4. Add the mane using the same method as for the dragon. Finally, give him a nice, sharp set of teeth. Drawing done!

Step 5. Ink him!

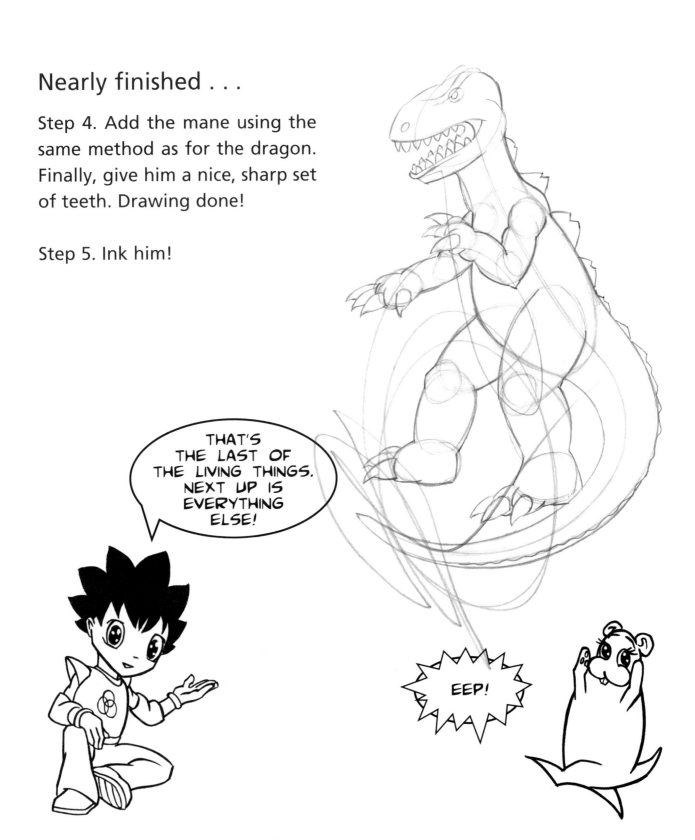

CHAPTER 7

Objects, Things, and Stuff

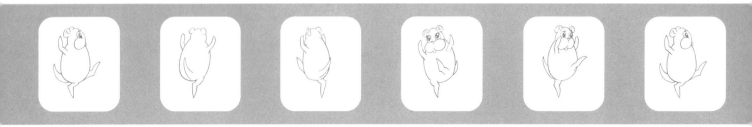

Drawing everyday objects

Geometric shapes

Unlike most living creatures, most everyday objects are made from just a few simple shapes.

A better understanding of these will allow us to draw just about everything, from boxes and books right up to cars and even large buildings! Let's start by looking at the shapes we need to know about.

Pictured on this page are the basic "building blocks" of objects you'd see every day.

Their names are:
1. cube
2. sphere
3. oblong
4. cylinder
5. wedge
6. pyramid

Make sure you know them by name, as we're going to start using them almost immediately!

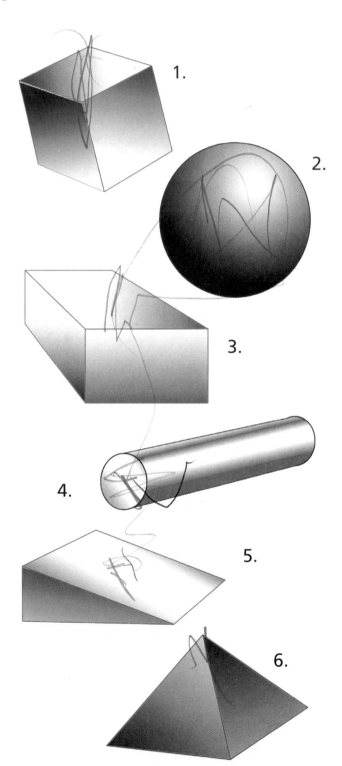

Below are a number of ordinary household items. They're all made out of the shapes from the previous page. See if you can work out which shapes make which item.

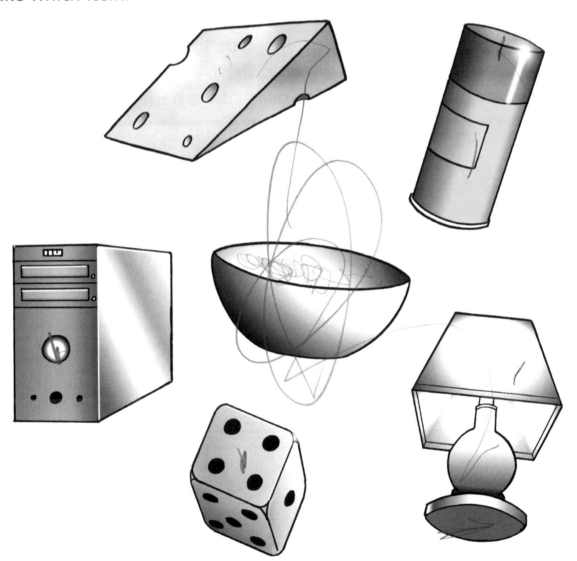

Get the idea? Before long, you'll be drawing your very own skyscrapers and hot-air balloons. But first, we need to have a quick look at something called *perspective*.

Perspective

We all know that the farther away something is, the smaller it looks. This is called *perspective*. So how do we use this to make our drawings better?

It all starts with knowing where the *horizon line* is. The horizon line is where the sky meets the surface of the earth. Imagine you are looking at the ocean. The place where the sea and the sky meet is the horizon line. Have a look at the simple picture below. See the horizon line?

The building on the right of the picture looks "right" because it follows the rules of perspective. Both the building and the sidewalk get smaller as they move toward the horizon line. The really important thing to know here is that those lines are all moving toward one point—something we call the *vanishing point.*

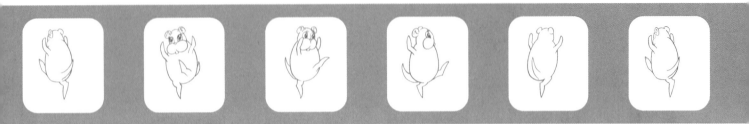

What is a vanishing point?

The gray lines in the drawing above show us where the sidewalk and building lines would end up joining if we carried them on to the horizon. The point where this happens is called the vanishing point. That's because it represents the place where the lines disappear over the horizon.

"H.L." = horizon line. "V.P." = vanishing point.

You'll probably want to refer back to this section to see how it applies to what's coming up next. Knowing perspective gives you an incredible amount of power to create convincing pictures.

The secrets of the sofa

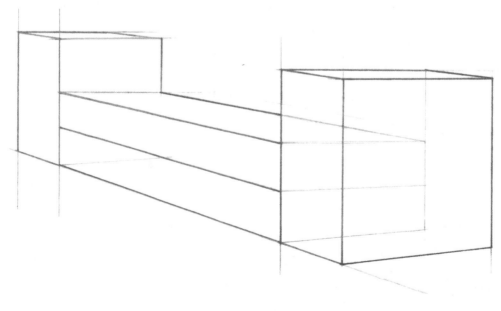

Step 1. The main part of the sofa is really just three oblongs. If we divide the middle oblong in half, we've got cushions as well!

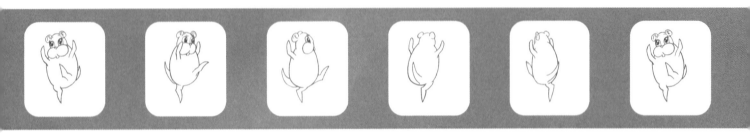

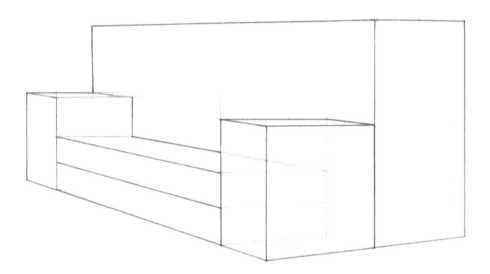

Step 2. One more large oblong will make up the back of the sofa.

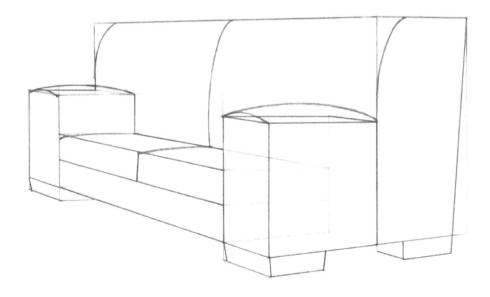

Step 3. Now for the refinements. Cut a thin wedge out of the back oblong to give us the angle shown. Cut the cushion oblong in half. Round off the hard edges of the back as shown. Add the padding on the arms. The feet are sawed-off, upside-down pyramids! We're done.

Draw a house

Planning permission

Step 1. This house is made from two oblongs that overlap.

Step 2. Make the two roof areas using two wedges.

Step 3. Erase your guidelines to make life easier for yourself!

Step 4. Add the windows and doors as shown.

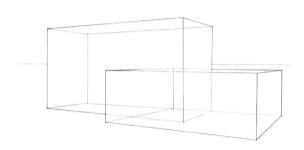

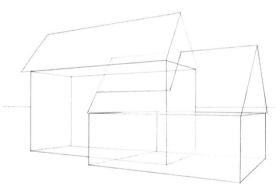

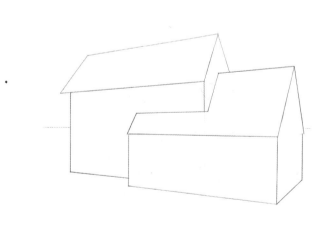

GET STEP ONE RIGHT AND THE REST IS QUITE EASY! CHECK PAGES 98-99 AGAIN IF IT GOES WRONG!

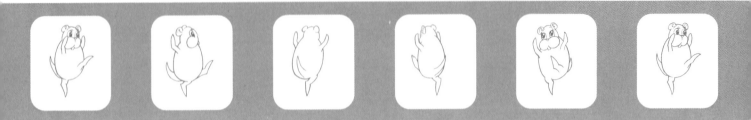

Step 5. Finish the details on the roof, windows, and door.

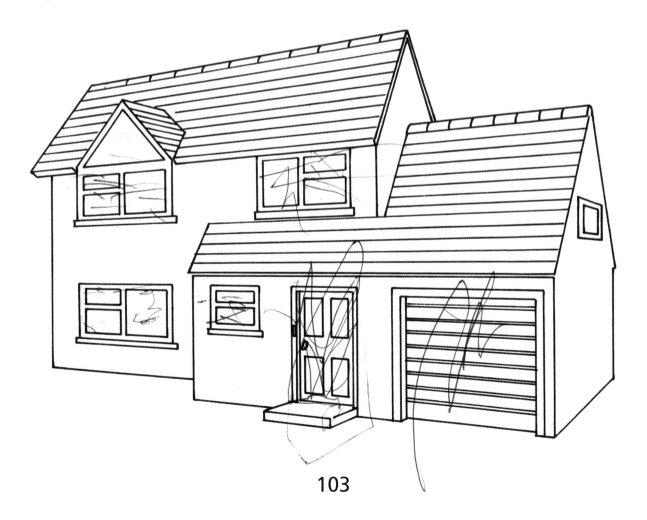

103

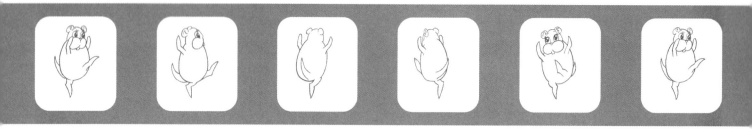

Draw a car

Hatchback or sedan

A car can be broken down to a simpler idea. A car is really just a small box on top of a larger box. Do this drawing to see what I mean.

Step 1. Draw the longer oblong first (the bottom one). Make the oblong on top about 2/3 as deep. Draw a line cutting this oblong in half and extending into the bottom one. Extend the ends of the top oblong into the body of the bottom one.

Step 2. Car wheels are short cylinders. But two circles, as shown, are fine for this drawing. Add the roofline, windows, and wheel arches.

Step 3. Add in the doors, handles, and fenders.

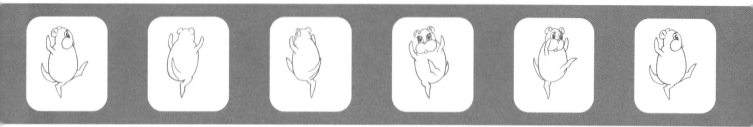

You can use this template to make many different types of car. Below is a sportier model, built on the same framework.

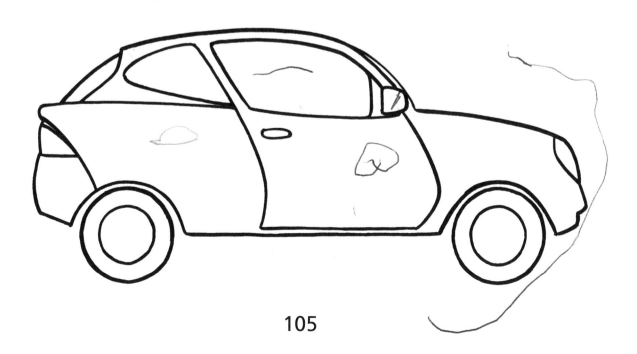

Drawing greenery

Trees

QUICK AND EASY WAYS TO FILL A PARK, GARDEN, OR MAZE!

Step 1. Make sure the trunk flares out toward the ground. To make our trees look more realistic, we'll use wobbly circles to imitate "clumps" of leaves.

Step 2. Loosely follow the circles with a "spiky" line.

106

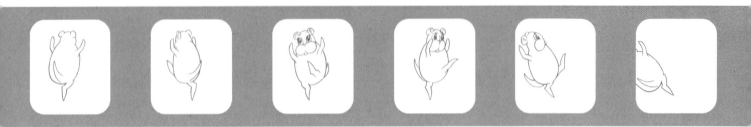

Hedges

Using this method, we can turn anything into a hedge. But for now, we'll stick with the common oblong hedge shape.

Step 1. Draw an oblong to the desired length and shape.

Step 2. Go over your original lines with an uneven line as shown.

Step 3. Add the "hedge holes." Be careful not to space these holes too regularly as it will look very unnatural.

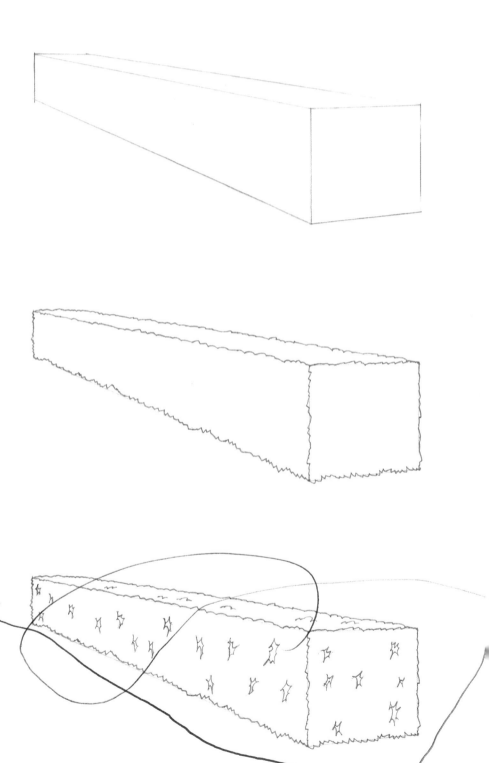

107

CHAPTER 8

The Big
Picture

Composition

Plan ahead!

In this section, we're going to take some of the things we've already learned how to draw and assemble them into one big picture. The first thing we need to do is get a good idea of what we want to draw in our heads. Our scene is going to include all of the items below. But how do we actually want to present them?

The clearer an idea is in our heads, the better chance we have of making a good composition. Once we've got an idea, we can start doing some sketches to see if it will work or not. The right preparation is essential. The more we plan ahead, the less we'll waste our time later on!

Preliminary sketch

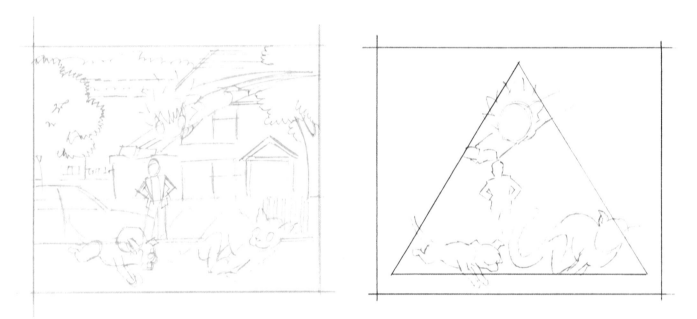

Have a look at the two images above. The one on the left is what is called a "thumbnail" sketch. This means it's a smaller, rougher version of what we want to draw. Thumbnails are a really good way to try out ideas. You shouldn't spend more than 5 to 10 minutes doing one, though. If it's not working out well, draw a fresh one and try to work out the problems in the one you did before.

On the right is a slightly strange-looking picture. But it tells us something very interesting about the composition. A large triangle in the center contains all the characters in our picture, and it's the characters that are the most important elements. This will help to give our image strength and a sense of structure. The viewer's mind will respond to "secret" shapes like this, although it's best not to make this too obvious in our pictures.

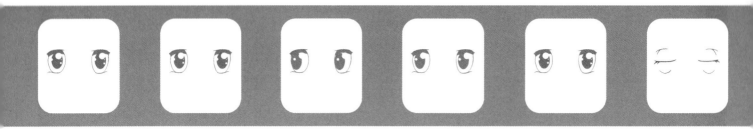

Drawing it for real

If we're happy with our sketch, we can start drawing the final picture.

Step 1. The first thing we need to do is loosely "lay out" the various objects and characters in our composition. Don't put in any detail at this stage!

Step 2. If we're happy that everything is in the right place, we can start to "firm up" the pencils on the characters. But don't bother with tiny details like eyeballs. We'll come to that stuff nearer the end.

Step 3. Now it's the turn of the nonliving things. This means the house, the car, the hedge and gate, the trees, the clouds, and the detail in the far background. Again, don't put every last detail in just yet.

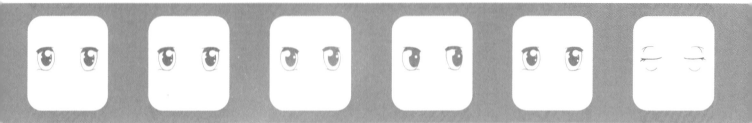

Step 4. This is the fine detail and "tightening up" stage. Finish the front door and window frames. Put in the last details on the car. Now you can put in those eye details and add whiskers to the cat. Add some speed lines to the flying figure of Mimimi. Finish the detail on the suit of the man looking on. We're nearly finished.

Step 5. This is the part where we fill in any black areas. You should always wait until the end to do this. Why? Large areas of solid pencil smear and smudge really easily. You'll pick it up on your hands as you draw and the whole picture will go a nasty shade of gray! Mimimi's hair, the man's hair, the dog's eyes and nose all need filling in. Any last details? How about some roof tiles? That's it!

Step 6. As with previous drawings, it is up to you whether you want to ink your drawing or not.

If you're not quite confident enough to do a completely different picture, why not simply rearrange the elements in this one? Experimentation leads to new discoveries.

117

CHAPTER 9

Create Your Own
Character

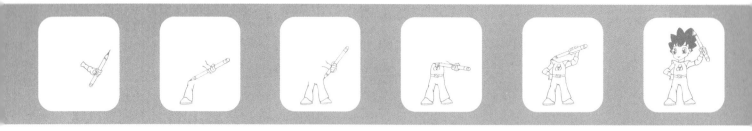

Body types

Little or large?

The first question we have to ask ourselves when creating a character is: "What kind of person is it?" They could be good, evil, silly, serious, or have any number of character traits.

Once the type of character we want to create has been decided upon, we then have to set about creating an appropriate body for him or her.

Cast your mind back to chapter six when we discussed body sizes. The big guy to our left quite closely resembles our giant on page 81. On the other hand, the small guy that he's making frightened is the exact opposite. This character was made using the same idea, but in reverse. Narrow shoulders, thin neck, skinny arms and legs. Most characters fall somewhere between these two body types. Let's have a look at the creation of someone we are already familiar with—the little guy who thinks he's the star of this book—Mimimi.

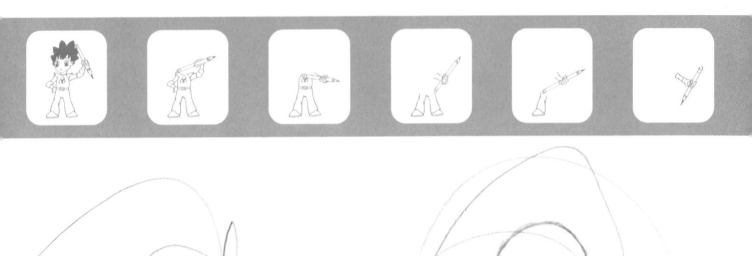

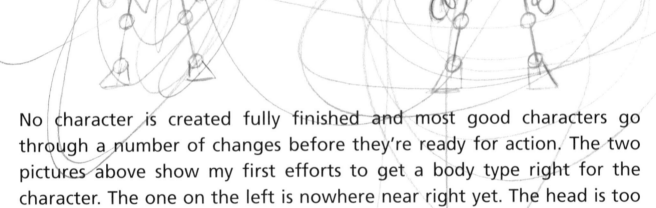

No character is created fully finished and most good characters go through a number of changes before they're ready for action. The two pictures above show my first efforts to get a body type right for the character. The one on the left is nowhere near right yet. The head is too small and the pelvic area isn't working the way I want it to.

Above right is an improvement. Moving the pelvis up into the body has given him a cuter look.

On the left is the body type that works—I've taken the best ideas from my original two sketches and made some other minor adjustments. Now we can go into more detail.

121

Prototypes

The first Mimimi

The pictures on this page are the first incarnation of the character. The body shape is more or less working, but very little else is! His face looks too evil and weird. His arms are too spindly and his hair needs improving.

Despite still being a long way off, the character is beginning to take shape. Now it is best to take our approach from the previous page. Use the good bits and throw out or improve the other stuff.

The elements are good, so let's have another go at rearranging them into something that feels right for the character.

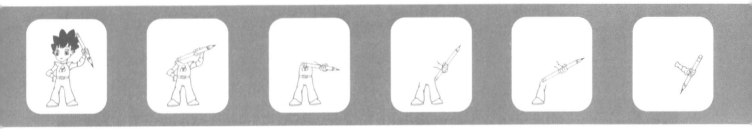

It's spot the difference time. There are some fairly radical changes to the character on the above left. I really like the fact that he's much cuter without being yucky. He's really close, but we need to have one more crack at it. Above right is the final design. Quite some evolution!

Now that we're happy with the character design, we can make sure the character is consistent no matter what angle we draw him from. This is done with the help of what's called a "turnaround" or "character rotation."

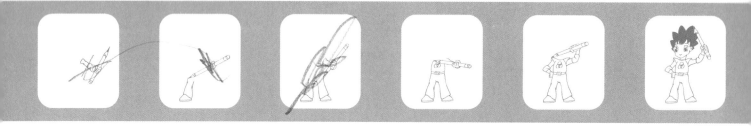

Mimimi turnaround

Covering all the angles

Character construction and "clean line" version.

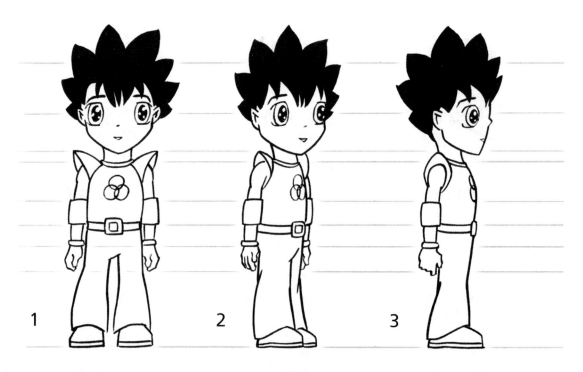

1 2 3

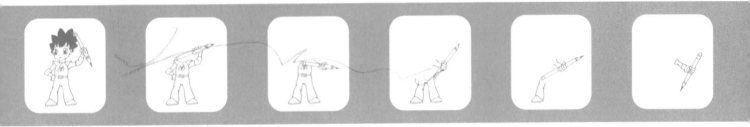

Note: Figure 6 is a mirror image of figure 4.

4   5   6

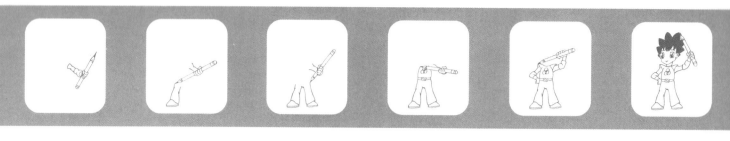

'MIMIMI' MODEL SHEET

HANDS & FEET

FEET POINT OUT SLIGHTLY WHEN STANDING

HEMLINE FOLLOWS SHAPE OF BOOT

FEET— SOLES

FOREFINGER SLIGHTLY AHEAD WHEN FORMING FIST SHAPE

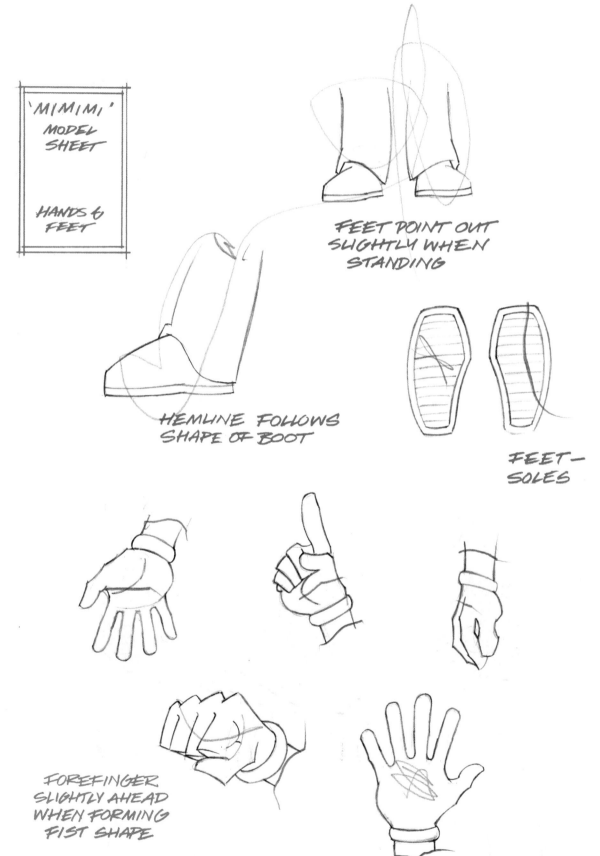

'MIMIMI' MODEL SHEET

ACTION/ EXPRESSION

HAIR LOOSELY FOLLOWS SHAPE OF HEAD

USE THIS SHAPE MOUTH WHEN SURPRISED, FRIGHTENED, ETC.

SHOULDERS— STARTS AT POINT WHERE NECK JOINS BODY

HEIGHT—TO CHINLINE

FOLLOWS BODYLINE

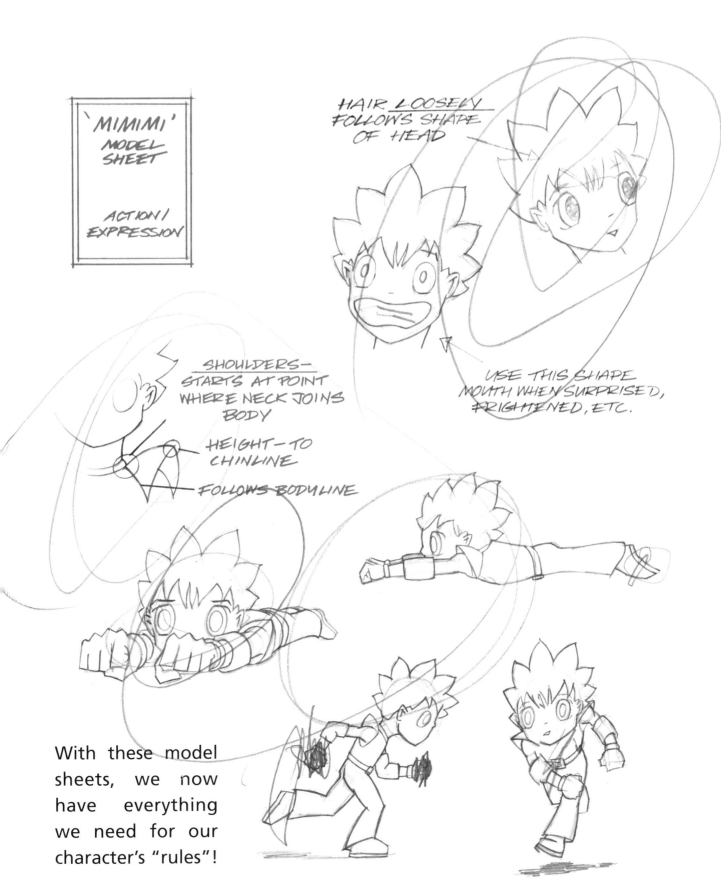

With these model sheets, we now have everything we need for our character's "rules"!

CHAPTER 10

Storytelling

131

132

Storytelling

THE DYNAMICS OF A STORY REVEALED

Let's break down these opening pages panel by panel to see what we can learn about the way they develop our story.

PANEL 1

This is called the "establishing shot." That's because its job is to establish or make clear the location where our story will take place.

This is nearly always the first thing you must tell your reader.

This panel is usually much bigger than most and often takes up the whole of the first page. This is partly to make an impact, but more importantly to make certain your reader is "in the picture."

PANELS 2 and 3

Now the reader knows where our story is taking place, but doesn't yet know when. The time of day is not always important in a story, but in this one it is. We'll make it absolutely clear what time of day it is through the next two panels.

There's nothing like a crowing cockerel to get the idea of early morning across so we'll use one.

Our next panel introduces one of the main characters, and also shows her in bed, yawning. We know she has just woken up (and not just gone to bed) because of our cockerel.

On the first page, we've done the following:
1. Set the location (including terrain and type of civilization).
2. Set the hour of day.
3. Introduced one of our main characters.

PANEL 4

Now for some drama: We know from the dialogue in the last panel of the previous page that our female character believes she is speaking to

someone. In this panel we need her to realize the person she thought she was speaking to is not there. This is very surprising to her and we need to communicate this. Using a wide panel, we can both focus on the object of her attention and show her surprise at realizing she's alone.

PANELS 5 and 6

These panels show how she reacts next—to immediately try to find the bed's usual occupant. They also give us the chance to show some more of the building we are currently in—a castle.

PANELS 7 and 8

These two panels introduce another character. We also find out the girl's name and that they are father and daughter. What else can we see? The father is doing up his boots, so the reader will assume he is about to go off somewhere.

In the background of panel 8 we can make out part of the staircase Kelka came down two panels ago. This helps link up the action and gives the reader more information about the castle.

137

PANELS 10 and 11

Scene change. We are introduced to Kelka's missing brother. In contrast to his father's reassuring words in panel 9 he is obviously in deep trouble. This allows us in on a secret. How long will it take Kelka's father to find out his fate? This unresolved question will bring additional suspense to our tale. Because we have been thrust straight into the scene without any introduction, Orin's confusion is *our* confusion.

PANELS 12 and 13

Another temporary mystery. We don't know at this stage exactly who or what Orin is looking at but it obviously disgusts him. By the mystery person's tone of voice, it's fairly obvious that he is Orin's captor.

There's quite a lot of tension in our story now. We are deliberately saving Orin's captor's identity for the next page. This will create more visual impact.

PANELS 14 and 15

The captor is revealed as a hideous manlike creature. Perhaps Orin's outburst was justified, but for the moment, we can't be sure.

In panel 15 we learn more about Orin's situation. Provided his captor isn't lying, his predicament seems to be going from bad to worse. There is a subtle threat from the captor before we switch scenes back again.

PANELS 17 and 18

At this point we switch scenes again to be confronted by a man using all his strength to try to move a stubborn beast. Any temporary confusion about where we are quickly disappears, though, as the familiar figure of Kelka appears in the doorway, placing us firmly back within the walls of the citadel. But what is this beast? The straining man seems to be implying that it belongs to Kelka. . . .

Where is this story heading?

We've managed to get a lot of information across in just a few short pages. But where does our story go from here? Hopefully you'll have had some ideas of your own. It's safe to say it already has the feeling, at least at the moment, of being a long, epic story. But that all depends on how it unfolds from here.

Picking up the baton

What questions are left unanswered? If we look at this, we immediately have some idea of where our story could go next.

Who is the ugly man-creature imprisoning the duke's son? And why would he want to do this? If we can find this character's *motivation*, this could propel us quite forcefully in any number of directions. Does he have a grudge against the wealthy people who live aboveground? Perhaps he is out to right some ancient wrong.

What is the beast that appears in the final two panels? What is Kelka's relationship to it? Could she really be its "owner"?

Is Kelka's father a good, noble man? He doesn't appear to be particularly affectionate toward his daughter. Why not?

Did Orin have it coming to him?

142

The end?

I hope this tiny taste of the start of a Manga story has given you some food for thought.

The right combination of characters and their interaction can cause a storyline to almost write itself. And a great plot can effortlessly generate great characters.

Actually, I myself want to know the answers to the questions from the previous pages.

Now where's that pencil. . . ?